The Perfect Picnic

By the Same Author:

The Perfect Picnic

Hilda Leyel

◪ **SQUARE PEG**

LONDON

Published by Square Peg 2011

2 4 6 8 10 9 7 5 3 1

Copyright © The Estate of Hilda Leyel 2011

Illustrations by Kate Bland

The Estate have asserted their right under the Copyright, Designs
and Patents Act 1988 to be identified as the author of this work

First published in Great Britain in 1936

This edition published in 2011 by
Square Peg
Random House, 20 Vauxhall Bridge Road,
London SWIV 2SA

www.rbooks.co.uk

Addresses for companies within The Random House Group Limited can be found at:
www.randomhouse.co.uk/offices.htm

The Random House Group Limited Reg. No. 954009

A CIP catalogue record for this book
is available from the British Library

ISBN 9780224086783

The Random House Group Limited supports The Forest Stewardship
Council (FSC), the leading international forest certification organisation. All our titles that
are printed on Greenpeace approved FSC certified paper carry the FSC logo. Our paper
procurement policy can be found at www.rbooks.co.uk/environment

Printed and bound in Germany by GGP Media GmbH, Pößneck

This little book was inspired by a picnic near Itchenor, given in the summer of 1935 by the owner of a white Peke to the owner of a white Alsatian.

"I commend white wine; it is less affected by movement and heat and more pleasantly exhilarating."

BRILLAT SAVARIN

"Then from his knapsack very calmly and contentedly he takes cold chicken and golden encrusted rolls, packed for him perchance by loving hands, and lays them conveniently by the wedge of Gruyere or Roquefort which is to be his whole dessert."

BRILLAT SAVARIN

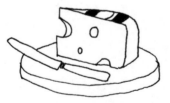

Contents

Preface

There are many people with cars who make a regular habit of spending Saturday or Sunday in the country—with a hamper of food they are independent of hotels and can eat their meals in any part of the country they choose.

To-day wide mouthed thermos flasks make it possible to arrange picnic food that is really delicious because not only hot or iced soups can have a place in the menu, but even curries, ragoûts and other casseroled dishes can be served steaming hot; or the meal can end with an iced sweet of some sort.

The art of arranging cold meals is to choose dishes that are better cold than they would be hot and it requires a certain amount of ingenuity and imagination to plan continuously meals of this kind because there are so few cookery books confined to cold dishes. It means as a rule wading through many books to find the few recipes that there are.

I think, therefore, that this little book and my *Cold Savoury*

Meals in the same series will be of great assistance to all those who have the choosing of food.

Most of the dishes I have chosen can be bought ready cooked from one of the large shops or pastrycooks if they are ordered the day before, but for those who wisely prefer to have the dishes made at home, I give the recipes.

The recipes for the cakes will be found in my book, *Cakes of England* in the same series.

Some of the food I have chosen in the following menus could be served hot and kept hot in a wide mouthed thermos but nearly everything would be better cold with the exception of the soups, some of which would be still better iced and kept very cold in the thermos.

If any of the dishes are out of season it is quite easy to substitute one from another menu. Strawberries, raspberries and asparagus have such a short season that no one has time to get tired of them and every menu when they are in season should include them.

Pies are as a rule much nicer cold than hot, but they must be made with plenty of jelly, and the savoury mousses too, must be surrounded by jelly.

It is better and more economical to buy the pastry for the pies from a good baker. Excellent puff pastry is sold by nearly every baker at a most moderate price.

Hard boiled eggs if they are to be eaten plain should be

shelled beforehand and packed in a wide mouthed screw jar.

A glass jar such as French plums are sold in is the best container for salads and many other things. Waxed cardboard cartons can also be used. Creams and soufflés should not be turned out of the moulds they are made in, and cakes and biscuits keep fresh in a tin. I have made a list a little farther on of what is needed for a practical picnic basket, with the approximate cost.

The expensively ready fitted baskets are not by any means the most useful and it is much more fun choosing the coloured cups and saucers and plates that please one's own fancy.

The most practical plates for meals are the white cardboard ones with waxed papers to fit, fluted at the edges so that they are heavy enough to stay on the plates which never get stained so that they can be used several times. The soiled papers are easily disposed of in some ditch, buried in the ground, and the knives are cleaned by being dug into the grass. In this way nothing is left to annoy the next comer or the generous owners of the property.

It is very distressing to see the countryside disfigured sometimes by paper bags and empty bottles and it spoils the enjoyment of all those to whom a picnic in the open air is a very real pleasure.

No one is too young or too old to delight in such a simple pleasure as a picnic in lovely surroundings and there is no more perfect way of spending a hot day. Sea, river, hills, woods or fields all make their appeal, and it is one of the best ways to get complete relaxation.

Hilda Leyel.
Shripney Manor,
Shripney,
Sussex.

Menus

Menu No. 1

Chicken pie.

Green pea and ham salad.

Chocolate mousse.

Cheddar cheese and crusty rolls.

23

Menu No. 2

Chicken liver terrine and French rolls.

Pea and potato salad.

Melon.

Flapjacks.

26

Menu No. 3
Glazed Cucumber.
Cream of Rabbit.
Spaghetti and Truffle Salad.
Apple cake.
27

Menu No. 4
Lobster cardinale.
Devilled lamb with nasturtium sauce.
Watercress and orange salad.
Cherry cake.
29

Menu No. 5
Cream of celery soup.
Foie gras pie.
Lettuce salad.
Lemon soufflé and pistachios.
32

Menu No. 6
Hard-boiled eggs.
Sausages and French mustard.
Ham and watercress salad.
Ripe pears and almond cakes.
36

Menu No. 7

Tomato cocktail.

Veal and ham pie.

Lettuce and cucumber salad.

Glacé grapes.

37

Menu No. 8

Hot artichoke soup.

Egg mayonnaise.

Bacon and broad bean salad.

Apricot cake.

Cheddar cheese and crusty rolls.

39

Menu No. 9

Mulligatawney soup.

Cold ham and potato salad.

Yorkshire parkin.

Cream cheese and celery biscuits.

41

Menu No. 10
Cottage crab.
Baked English casserole.
French bean salad and mousse of eggs.
Lemon cake.
42

Menu No. 11
Smoked salmon.
Veal loaf and cauliflower salad.
Polenta and orange cake.
Gruyere cheese and water biscuits.
44

Menu No. 12
Potted grouse.
Cold chicken.
Compôte of peppers.
Fruit salad.
46

Menu No. 13
Stuffed pimentos.
Roast pork and sauce Robert.
Potatoes in jackets.
Cream-cheese, black olives and cream crackers.
47

Menu No. 14
Hot almond soup.
Chicken with poulette sauce.
Asparagus and cucumber salad.
Strawberries and cream.
49

Menu No. 15
Spiced pressed beef.
Beetroot and cabbage salad.
Brandied peaches.
Goats' cheese and wholemeal rolls.
51

Menu No. 16
Hot potato soup.
Marinade of halibut.
Cucumber and gherkin salad.
Coffee cake.
Cheshire cheese and oat cakes.
53

Menu No. 17
Lobster cream.
Pigeon pie.
Orange and celery salad.
Rice cake.
55

Menu No. 18
An excellent fish pie.
Cold tongue.
Egg, watercress and nut salad.
Grapefruit salad with Kirsch.
56

Menu No. 19
Game terrine with red currant jelly.
Beef and horseradish sauce.
Spiced beetroot, potatoes in jackets.
Fruit cake.
58

Menu No. 20
Purée of smoked haddock with tartare sauce.
Chicken and bread sauce.
Chinese orange salad.
Chocolate soufflé and Devonshire cream.
60

Menu No. 21

Hot green pea soup.

Salad of curried rice and olives and cucumber.

Pineapple cake.

Roquefort cheese and oat biscuits.

62

Menu No. 22

Eggs with anchovy butter.

Rabbit pie and catsup.

Watercress salad.

Melon.

64

Menu No. 23

Roast duck and apple sauce.

Green pea, orange and beetroot salad.

Ginger cake.

Goats' cheese and Bath Olivers.

66

Menu No. 24

Cold consommé.

Chicken and bread sauce.

Watercress, beetroot and nasturtium salad.

Torone and quince jam.

Camembert cheese, olives and brioches.

67

Menu No. 25

Sausages and French mustard

Beetroot salad.

Apple flan.

Gorgonzola cheese and wholemeal scones.

70

Menu No. 26

Chicken liver mousse and caraway straws.

Ham with Cumberland sauce.

Spaghetti and green pepper salad.

Raspberries and cream.

71

Menu No. 27
Crab tartlets.
Macédoine of vegetables.
Pickled peaches.
Cheddar cheese, green butter and water biscuits.
73

Menu No. 28
Asparagus soup.
Salmon loaf.
Spinach soufflé.
Fresh peaches and cream.
75

Menu No. 29
Foie gras tartlets.
Cold beef with horseradish sauce.
Sweet potatoes in jackets.
Cherry jam and fresh English household bread.
77

Menu No. 30
Cantaloupe melon.
Cold curry and rice.
Tomato, coconut and olive salad.
Lemon pie.
78

Menu No. 31

Hot carrot soup.

Jamaica mould and savoury grapefruit salad.

Seed cake.

Stilton cheese and wholemeal bread.

80

Menu No. 32

Prawn patties.

Beef salad and asparagus soufflé.

Black currant pie and Devonshire cream.

82

Menu No. 33

Marinated herrings.

Knap pie and asparagus.

Spiced plum cake and salted almonds.

84

Menu No. 34

Hot consommé and pirogs.

Pressed veal and mousse of vegetables.

Meringues.

Cheddar cheese and oatcakes.

85

Menu No. 35
Salmon served in lemons.
Partridge pie
Galantine of vegetable.
Anchovy biscuits.
87

Menu No. 36
Hot onion soup.
Chicken and leek pie.
Ham, beetroot and pea salad.
Orange salad with Kirsch.
89

Menu No. 37
Shrimp pie.
Beetroot and apple salad.
Treacle tart.
91

Menu No. 38
Anchovy tartines.
Ham loaves with spiced prunes.
Tarragon, chervil and lettuce salad.
Griddlecakes with honey.
93

Menu No. 39
Crab soufflé.
Pheasant with tartare sauce.
Lettuce and cucumber salad.
Coffee soufflé.
94

Menu No. 40
Eggs stuffed with sardines.
Dutch roll and orange salad.
Pears in brandy.
Blue Cheshire cheese and cobs.
96

Menu No. 41
Hot tomato soup.
Veal with tunny fish and anchovies and egg pie.
Fruit salad.
98

Menu No. 42
Crab ravigote.
Fricandeau of veal.
Grapefruit and walnut salad.
Charlotte Russe with strawberries.
100

Menu No. 43

Quiche Lorraine.

Tomato and cucumber salad.

Seed cake.

102

Menu No. 44

Mousse of chicken.

Pork chops with apple purée.

Beetroot, horseradish and celery salad.

Madeira cake.

103

Menu No. 45

Wild mushroom soup.

Roman pie.

Brandy snaps filled with vanilla cream.

Caraway cheese and water biscuits.

105

Menu No. 46

Devilled crab.

Beef and pimento salad.

Marmalade tart.

Stilton cheese and household bread.

107

Menu No. 47
Prawn salad.
Mutton pie with a puree of peppers hash and
hot haricot beans.
Bananas with rum.
108

Menu No. 48
Mousse of haddock.
Avocado pears.
Devilled chicken and tomato jelly.
Walnut cake.
111

Menu No. 49
Fishchowder soup.
Spiced loaf with glazed cucumber.
Stewed red currants and cream of tapioca.
113

Menu No. 50
Mousse of eggs.
Smoked sausages and sauerkraut.
Stuffed olives and potato salad.
Apple pie and Devonshire cream.
115

Menu No. 51
Truite au bleu.
Indian pie with rice.
Apple soufflé and gingerbread.
117

Menu No. 52
Asparagus in French rolls.
Grouse and pickled plums.
Lettuce salad and cucumber.
Caramel soufflé.
119

Menu No. 53
Faggot loaves.
Daube of lamb and spiced prunes.
Salad of pineapple and grapefruit.
Strawberry short cake.
121

Menu No. 54
Cold vegetable soup.
Pheasant with slices of foie gras.
Potato salad.
Banana ice cream.
124

Menu No. 55
Pâté de volaille.
Vegetable Macédoine.
Strawberry soufflé.
127

Menu No. 56
Spiced oysters.
Chicken cream.
Sweet pepper salad.
Camembert cheese and Bath Olivers.
128

Menu No. 57
Hot beetroot soup.
Partridges in cream.
Salad of mint leaves and beans.
Butterscotch pie.
130

Menu No. 58
Hot Piedmontese soup.
Lamb chops with potato salad.
Caramel nut ice.
Gruyere cheese and water biscuits.
132

Recipes

Note

The recipes which follow are given in the same order as the Menus listed in the previous pages. However certain Menu items, which are either shop-bought or self-evidently assembled, such as various cheese and pudding courses, do not have a recipe given below.

Menu 1

Chicken Pie

Skin a good chicken and cut into joints. Bone it carefully and highly season the boned flesh with cayenne, salt, pounded mace and nutmeg; line a pie dish with a thin pastry and spread over it a layer of sausage meat which has been made into a paste with a few spoonfuls of water and to which a little finely shredded shallot has been added. On the top of this place closely together some of the boned pieces of chicken. Then put another layer of sausage meat and continue in the same way till the dish is nearly full, then fill up with stock or water in which a little gelatine has been dissolved.

Roll out a thin pastry about half an inch thick to fit over the top. Take off the superfluous pastry round the edges and make an incision in the top of the pie, and decorate the top with pastry cut into leaves. Glaze the whole pie with a brush dipped in yolk of eggs and bake in a good oven from an hour and a half to two hours.

To make the pastry:

Sift a pound of good flour and rub into it with the tips of the fingers eight ounces of butter, then add a small saltspoonful of salt and make into a firm paste with the yolks of two eggs well beaten and mixed with less than a quarter of a pint of water. It should be strained before it is added to the flour and butter.

Roll out into an oblong shape and cut off sufficient to line the inside of the pie dish. Roll it out to about a sixth or an eighth of an inch in thickness. Then cut off another piece, roll it to a quarter of an inch, wet the rim of the pie dish and lay it round the edge. If it is necessary to join it, do not let it overlap but make a proper join by adding a little water. After this is done, damp it slightly on the top, roll out the top of the pie to the thickness of half an inch, and place it over the top of the dish, pressing the edges to give it easy room over the meat, so that it will not stretch in the cooking and spoil the appearance. With a sharp knife cut off the superfluous edges. Trim it neatly and slit a hole in the top of the pie.

The leaves are made by cutting a strip of pastry about an inch and a half wide and cutting it across diagonally in the shape of a diamond and with the back of the knife the veins of the leaves are marked. In putting on the leaves, care must be taken not to cover up the slit or hole at the top of the pie.

Green Pea and Ham Salad

Cook some new green peas in the usual way. Drain them and allow them to get cold. Then put them into a salad bowl.

Chop up a few pieces of cooked lean ham very fine, add to the peas. Season with pepper and salt, oil and a little vinegar and sprinkle over the top some finely grated horseradish.

Chocolate Mousse

Put into a double saucepan two and a half ounces of good chocolate (grated), two ounces of sugar, half a pint of water, half an ounce of gelatine, the thin rind and juice of half a lemon. Heat until the gelatine and sugar are dissolved. Let it cool, and flavour with vanilla. When cold, but before it sets, add it spoonful by spoonful to the whites of two eggs. Beat till very stiff and pour into a mould to set.

Menu 2

Chicken Liver Terrine

Take some fresh pork and veal and chicken livers. Mince them, mix with pepper and salt and pass through a sieve or pound them in a mortar.

Mix a glass of sherry with them, then line a game pie dish with fat bacon, put a layer of the mince, thin strips of bacon and more mince. Put bay leaves on the top, cover with more bacon fat and bake in a tin of water for two hours. When cold cover the top with meat jelly.

Pea and Potato Salad

Choose waxy potatoes, cook them and chop them into small pieces; cook some green peas and let them drain well, and freely shred a stick or more of horseradish.

Then put the peas and potato into a salad bowl and mix the horseradish with it. Cover with the following sauce:

Beat two eggs in a double saucepan, add a saltspoonful of salt, a teaspoonful of mixed mustard, two dessertspoonfuls of sugar, an ounce of butter, four tablespoonfuls of milk and three tablespoonfuls of vinegar.

Stir till thick and then pour over the salad.

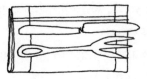

Menu 3

Glazed Cucumber

Choose a cucumber without seeds, split it and divide into pieces about three inches, and then put into a pan with an ounce of butter and about three-quarters of a pint of good stock, a pinch of salt and a teaspoonful of sugar. Do not cover, but cook gently, shaking them occasionally to prevent them burning.

Season well and in about half an hour they should be well glazed.

Serve cold.

Cream of Rabbit

Bone a young rabbit, chop the flesh finely and put it through a mincer, and pound it in a mortar till smooth. Work in a raw egg, season it well with cayenne, salt and pepper. Pass the mixture through a sieve, then put it into a saucepan with some good white stock, add a little flour and stir till it is of the consistency of cream.

Serve cold with a border of tiny white onions and an outer border of cold Patna rice.

Spaghetti and Truffle Salad

Cook the spaghetti, drain it, season it well with pepper and salt and chop the truffles and mix with it.

Cover with a good tomato sauce.

Instead of truffles, cold chopped mushrooms could be used or some chopped chicken liver cooked in stock or water.

Menu 4

Lobster Cardinale

The lobsters must be carefully chosen. They should be heavy in proportion to their size. As a rule the cock lobster is considered better in flavour than the hen, but for this dish at any rate one hen will be required for the coral which is needed for the sauce. The male is usually narrower in the tail than the female.

A white encrusted shell substance on the outside indicates that the lobster is not young.

Split the lightly boiled lobsters with a very sharp knife right down the middle of the back from the head to the tail. Remove the vein-like intestine from the centre of the tail, the stomach which will be found in the head, and the spongy gills.

Remove the meat without breaking it (put the coral on one side), crack the large claws, remove the meat from them without breaking it and leave the claws themselves as whole as possible for decoration.

Arrange the meat in neat pieces at the bottom of the dish on a bed of lettuce. Then make the following sauce:—

Take one ounce of butter and the same of flour, half a pint of fish stock, half a gill of cream. Season with salt and cayenne and a teaspoonful of lemon juice. Mix the butter and flour in a saucepan over the fire, then add the fish stock, stirring carefully.

Pound the coral of the lobster with a little butter, pass it through a sieve and add it to the butter, flour and stock, stirring all the time till it thickens. Then put to one side and presently add the cream, lemon, cayenne and salt and pour over the lobster. Decorate the dish with lettuce, cucumber and the claws, large and small, of the lobsters.

Devilled lamb

Cut as many slices as required from an underdone shoulder or leg of lamb, cutting them about half an inch thick. Then spread them with the following mixture made into a paste.

Take a tablespoonful of dry mustard, a tablespoonful of chutney, a tablespoonful of salad oil, a quarter of a teaspoonful of sugar, a few drops of Lea & Perrin's Worcester Sauce and pepper to taste.

Then cook them in a tin in the oven for seven or eight minutes. Serve cold on a bed of watercress, with nasturtium sauce.

Nasturtium Sauce

Melt six tablespoonfuls of butter and add the same of flour, mixing into a paste. Season with salt and pepper and, when smooth, add one and a half cups of water and cook till thick, stirring all the time. Then add gradually another three table-spoonfuls of butter and the same of nasturtium seeds, pick-led or fresh.

Watercress and Orange Salad

Wash the watercress and drain it in a wire basket. Peel the oranges, carefully remove all trace of the inner white skin and then with a sharp knife cut them into long triangular thin slices, removing all the pith and pips. They must not be jagged or untidy.

Divide the watercress with the fingers into sprays and put first a layer of watercress and then of orange till it is completed. Pour over the salad a dressing of oil, vinegar, pepper and salt and decorate the top with shredded horseradish or powdered nuts.

Menu 5

Cream of Celery Soup

Wash a good head of celery, then finely shred all the white and young green part. Put into a pan of boiling water and cook it for ten minutes, then strain it into a colander and put it under the cold tap.

Then melt an ounce of butter in a pan, add the celery and let it cook slowly for a quarter of an hour.

Mix an ounce of cornflour with two pints of water; add it to the celery and stir it till it boils and thickens. Add pepper and salt and a pinch of onion salt, and leave it to simmer for about an hour.

Rub through a sieve, return the purée to the pan and reheat it.

Beat up the yolks of two eggs with half a pint of milk, strain this into the soup and stir till nearly boiling but do not let it actually boil. Add an ounce of butter before removing from the fire and pour into the thermos flask.

Foie Gras Pie

A Périgord pie is an expensive dish whether made at home or bought ready made.

It is also an ambitious dish for the average cook to attempt, but this is how to make it.

Bone three pigeons and cut the flesh into small pieces and put through a mincing machine. Season with pepper and salt, mixed spice, minced parsley and young onions. Take a pound of truffles—hash the small ones and pound them with the livers of the pigeons and a fat goose liver or the fat livers of poultry—in a mortar. Add raw egg by degrees to make into a suitable paste.

Season the whole very highly; grease a raised pie mould and line it with the pastry rolled out to about a quarter of an inch.

Be careful to press the pastry into every part of the mould and to keep it to the same thickness. Trim off the edges with a pair of scissors. Then spread the paste with the pounded liver and truffles and fill up the centre with the pigeon to which should be added half a pound of minced veal and half a pound of breadcrumbs and the rest of the truffles.

Cover with more of the pounded liver and some whole truffles. Wet round the inner edge of the pastry lining, and roll out the trimmings of pastry to form a lid. Lay it on, pressing the edges together, and trim round with scissors.

Make a slit in the centre, brush over with beaten egg and decorate with leaves made from the pastry.

Place the pie on a baking tin in a moderate oven till the top crust is cooked and browned.

Then cover with paper, reduce the heat and cook for a further hour or so till tender.

Take out of the oven and, when cooler, lift off the tin. Fill up the pie with jelly stock made from the trimmings and liver of the pigeons with a little added gelatine.

To make the pastry:

Sieve a pound of flour into a basin with a teaspoonful of salt and rub in a quarter of a pound of butter and a quarter of a pound of lard. Then make into a paste with the yolk of an egg mixed with a little water.

Turn on to a floured board, knead lightly with the hands till smooth. Cover over and lay aside till wanted.

Lettuce Salad

Choose round lettuces with good hearts. Strip off the outer leaves after washing the lettuces well in cold water and draining them in a wire basket. Only use the inner leaves and do not divide them—use them whole. Dry them in a cloth.

Then put them into a bowl which has been smeared with a clove of garlic, and pour over them just before serving a dressing made of twice the quantity of olive oil to that of tarragon vinegar, and pepper and salt to taste.

Lemon Soufflé

Beat the yolks of four eggs with six ounces of castor sugar over hot water till thick. Then add four sheets of gelatine dissolved in a little water. Whisk till cool.

Add the strained juice and finely grated rind of two large lemons. Whip till stiff half a pint of cream, and fold in the white of the four eggs also stiffly whipped.

Decorate with pistachio nuts.

Menu 6

Fried Sausages

Cook the sausages in the usual way, but they must be very thoroughly browned all over. This means very slow cooking and constant turning. Every part of the sausage should be covered with a thick brown crust.

Ham and Watercress Salad

Prepare the watercress as for Watercress and Orange Salad and place in a salad bowl.

Chop finely some cold lean ham and mix with the watercress. Then prepare a salad dressing of oil and vinegar, pepper and salt, and sprinkle over the top of the salad.

Menu 7

Tomato Cocktail

Add to a cup of strained tomato juice a teaspoonful of finely chopped onion. Press through a fine sieve and mix with a tablespoonful of lemon juice, a tablespoonful of wine vinegar, a teaspoonful of finely chopped celery or half a teaspoonful of celery seed; half a small bay leaf and a level tablespoonful of sugar.

Let it stand two hours in a cool place, then strain and put in the refrigerator.

Veal and Ham Pie

Cut into small pieces a pound of lean veal from which all the skin has been removed, a quarter of a pound of lean ham and bacon, cutting it into neat strips. Mix together with some finely chopped parsley, pepper and salt and the thinly grated rind of half a lemon and a little water.

Arrange in the dish with slices of hard-boiled egg and cover with parsley. When the pie is baked, heat some good jelly stock and pour it through the hole at the top of the pie with a funnel. Leave it to get cold.

For the pastry, see Chicken Pie.

Lettuce and Cucumber Salad

Wash the lettuce and leave it in a wire basket to drain. Then dry it further by wrapping it in a clean towel and patting it.

Take off the outer leaves and use the inner ones, breaking them with the fingers. Arrange them in the salad bowl.

Slice part of a cucumber after peeling it very thinly, and mix it with the lettuce. Then add a few chopped gherkins and dress the salad with oil and vinegar, pepper and salt.

Glacé Grapes

Put two teacupfuls of white sugar into an enamel saucepan with a cup of boiling water and half a teaspoonful of cream of tartar. Heat to boiling water. Boil without stirring until syrup begins to discolour, which is 310 degrees F. Wash off the sugar that adheres to the sides of the pan. Remove saucepan from fire and place in larger pan of cold water to instantly stop boiling. Take the grapes in small clusters from the bunch and dip in the syrup and remove to oiled paper.

Menu 8

Hot Artichoke Soup

Pare quickly a pound of Jerusalem artichokes and put them immediately into milk to prevent them turning black. Boil them till soft in half a pint of milk and a pint of water. Strain through a wire sieve. Put back into the pan, season with salt and pepper and add another half-pint of milk and a lump of butter. Stir with a wooden spoon and allow to boil for seven minutes. Thicken with a little flour.

Mayonnaise of Eggs with Tartare Sauce

Hard boil the number of eggs required. Shell them and cut them in half lengthways.

Wash a lettuce with a good heart to it and put in a wire basket to drain. Then gather it into a cloth to dry it further.

Pull it to pieces with the hands, discarding the outer leaves if they are unsightly.

Make a bed of the leaves for the eggs to rest on and put a handful of mustard and cress under each one. Decorate the dish with sliced beetroot, shredded horseradish and watercress. Then pour over the eggs a sauce tartare.

Sauce Tartare

Make a mayonnaise sauce in the ordinary way with oil and vinegar, adding the oil drop by drop and the yolk of an egg and beating it till thick. Then add a little mustard and enough white vinegar to flavour it without making it too thin, and finally add a handful of chopped parsley, gherkins and tarragon.

Bacon and Broad Bean Salad

Choose a nice piece of bacon (the back), half lean and half fat. Cook it very slowly in boiling water with the lid on, allowing half an hour to each pound.

Add a cupful of vinegar and six cloves to the water in which it is boiled, and when the cooking is over leave the bacon in it all night to absorb the flavour. The bacon should be so well cooked that it melts in the mouth. The next day brush the top with egg and spread breadcrumbs over it.

It may not look so nice as it would if less well cooked, but the taste is infinitely better.

Let the bacon boil quickly for the first ten minutes of the cooking and afterwards very slowly.

Remove the outer shell of the broad beans and cook as much as is required. Drain well and allow to get cool. Then place in a salad bowl and mix with cold peas. Add pepper and salt. Cover with an oil and vinegar dressing and sprinkle with chopped parsley.

Menu 9

Mulligatawney Soup

Cut an onion in rings and an ounce of ham into dice. Put an ounce of butter in a frying pan and fry the onion and ham in it till golden brown, then add one turnip cut in small pieces, part of a carrot sliced and a small apple sliced, and after that a teaspoonful of good curry powder and half a teaspoonful of curry paste and a quart of stock. Leave them to simmer for an hour, then strain through a hair sieve. Put back into the pan and add a tablespoonful of flour mixed with a little cold water and stir till the soup boils and thickens.

Potato Salad

Choose small waxy potatoes and boil a pound in their skins. When sufficiently cooked cut into slices while warm. Put into a bowl and cover with olive oil and a glass of white wine; add salt and pepper and seasoning and sprinkle with very finely chopped parsley and shallot.

Menu 10

Cottage Crab

Boil a pound of good firm fish, either hake or skate, flake it while hot and free it from bone and skin. Leave it to cool.

Lay a ring of it round the dish in which it will be served, and outside it a ring of thinly sliced cucumber, and outside that a ring of small lettuce leaves. Fill the inner ring with the following mixture.

Put into a small saucepan four ounces of picked shrimps, shelled and chopped, two eggs and a lump of butter, cayenne pepper and salt to taste. Stir in a double saucepan till thick and then add to the centre of the fish ring. Then put a ring of cooked Patna rice between the cucumber and the lettuce and sprinkle it with chopped red pepper.

Baked English Casserole

Wash two young rabbits, cut into joints and place them in a casserole. Sprinkle over and round them stuffing made of half a pound of breadcrumbs, a tablespoonful of chopped onion, two tablespoonfuls of chopped parsley, a tablespoonful of mixed herbs, a tablespoonful of chopped candied peel, a good pinch of pepper and an egg. Lay on top of the stuffing half a pound of bacon cut into thin rashers. Pour over the whole half a cupful of milk, put on a lid and bake in the oven for two and a half hours.

This is one of the dishes that would be better hot and that would go easily into a wide mouthed thermos.

Salad of French Beans

Slice and cook the French beans in the usual way. Put into a colander to drain and then place in the salad bowl. Season well and pour over them a dressing of oil and vinegar, and sprinkle with paprika.

Mousse of Eggs

Put through a sieve the yolks of four or more hard-boiled eggs and chop the whites separately. Then add to the yolks enough Lea & Perrin's Worcester Sauce, tomato ketchup and anchovy sauce to taste, and three tablespoonfuls of aspic jelly. Then add the whites of eggs and half a pint of cream lightly whipped. Put into a mould and place in the refrigerator. Run a little more aspic over the top and turn out on to a bed of lettuce.

Menu 11

Smoked Salmon

This can be bought from any good grocer. It should be very thinly sliced and eaten on French rolls, sliced and buttered.

Veal Loaf

Chop very finely three pounds of veal taken from the leg, and four ounces of pork. Add three teaspoonfuls of salt and a teaspoonful of black pepper, a dash of cayenne and a pinch of powdered cloves; also a breakfastcupful of breadcrumbs. Beat up two good eggs and make the whole into a dough with them. Pour into a wetted mould. Cover closely and steam for two hours.

Then put the mould into the oven for a few minutes to dry with the door open. When cold turn out, cut in slices and decorate with sprigs of parsley and slices of transparent lemon.

Cauliflower Salad

Cook one or more cauliflowers in the usual way and then leave them in a colander to drain.

Divide the flower into small branches and place these in a salad bowl.

Season well with pepper, salt and cayenne and pour over the salad the following sauce.

Beat two eggs in a double pan. Add a small teaspoonful of salt, a teaspoonful of mixed mustard, two dessertspoonfuls of sugar, an ounce of butter, four tablespoonfuls of milk and three tablespoonfuls of vinegar. Stir over boiling water till it thickens. Then pour over the salad or bottle and pour it over before it is served.

Menu 12

Potted Grouse

Remove all the meat from the bones of a cold roasted grouse, and put them in a small saucepan with a glass of sherry, a glass of mushroom catsup, four shallots, a bay leaf, thyme and small piece of ham or bacon and one and a half pints of good gravy. Boil this down to a glaze and strain it into a basin. First chop and then pound all the meat into a mortar, add the glaze, four ounces of clarified butter, salt and cayenne. Pound all together and fill small pots, cover with clarified butter.

Compôte of Peppers

Remove the seeds from twelve red and twelve green peppers, cutting them in half first.

Then chop them up rather finely and add twelve onions also finely chopped. Cover them with boiling water and leave them for five minutes.

Then drain them and add four level tablespoonfuls of salt. Bring to the boiling point a cupful of sugar and a pint and a half of vinegar. Boil for five minutes, pour over the peppers and fill the jars.

Menu 13

Stuffed Pimentos

Take green or red pimentos or some of each. Cut off the tops, chop them up and fry them in butter till soft and brown with two sliced onions. Season with salt and pepper and add a teacupful of water, two tablespoonfuls of tomato juice and a teacupful of half-cooked and well-drained Patna rice. Add a little butter and strain the sauce, keeping aside the liquid that comes from it.

Stuff the pimentos with this mixture and cook them in

the oven in a casserole with the liquid poured over until soft, about fifteen or twenty minutes.

Roast Pork

Choose a nice piece of neck with the outer skin or crackle.

Put it into a hot oven for the first five minutes and then lower the heat and cook very slowly, basting well till finished. Leave it to cool. This should be served in one piece and is very delicious with cold apple sauce and Sauce Robert.

The dish should be decorated with sprigs of parsley.

Sauce Robert

Chop up several onions and fry them in two ounces of butter in a closed pan for fifteen minutes. Then remove the lid, stir in a dessertspoonful of flour with a wooden spoon, and when it has become soft and brown, pour over it half a pint of hot stock. Season it with a teaspoonful of made mustard, a teaspoonful of red wine vinegar and salt and pepper to taste. Reduce the sauce a little by further boiling, and stir all the time.

Potatoes in Jackets

Take as many large potatoes as are required. Cook them in their skins in the oven and, when cool, cut off the tops, keeping them carefully, and scoop out all the potato.

Mix in a bowl with pepper, salt, butter and a little milk into a smooth purée.

Half fill the cases and break an egg into each. Put into the oven to set the eggs, and then fill up with the purée and put on the ends and serve cold.

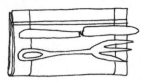

Menu 14

Hot Almond Soup

Melt an ounce of butter in a pan, add six ounces of minced onions, fry till yellow and stir in an ounce of flour; when well blended, moisten with some white haricot broth and add a breakfastcupful of ground sweet almonds, and a pint of white haricot broth, or what is left of it, by degrees. Let this come to the boil. Skim and simmer gently for half an hour. Pass through a hair sieve, warm up and add a gill of cream with which the yolk of an egg has been mixed after it has been taken from the fire.

Chicken with Poulette Sauce

Boil a chicken and, when cold, remove the skin and bone. Cut into neat pieces. Season well with pepper and salt. Arrange in a dish and pour over it a poulette sauce.

Garnish the dish with lettuce, chopped gherkins and sliced beetroot, and decorate the top with paprika.

Poulette Sauce

Make a béchamel sauce and add after it has been cooked, a yolk of egg diluted in a little vinegar. The sauce must not boil again and must be poured over the chicken before it sets.

Asparagus and Cucumber Salad

Cook the asparagus in the usual way and drain carefully. Slice the cucumber after peeling it. Sprinkle it with salt and leave it for an hour in a soup plate. Cut off the heads of the asparagus as far as they are edible. Then drain the cucumber and arrange it at the bottom of the dish with the asparagus on top and pour over the whole a cold Mousseline sauce.

Mousseline Sauce

Break into a breakfast cup the yolks of two eggs and add a little lemon juice and a drop of cold water and two ounces of butter broken into small pieces.

Stand it in a bowl of very hot water and stir it quickly with a wooden spoon till it becomes like cream. The sauce must on no account be allowed to get hot or it will curdle.

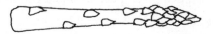

Menu 15

Spiced Pressed Beef

Take four to six pounds of brisket of beef which has been in brine for a few days. Put it into a large saucepan of warm water with two carrots, two onions, a turnip, all chopped fine, twenty peppercorns bruised and six cloves also bruised.

Let it come to the boil and simmer gently for at least four hours or until it leaves the bone quite easily.

Slip out the bones, roll it in a cloth and press well between two dishes with heavy weights on the top. Next day dissolve

half an ounce of meat glaze in a tablespoonful of hot water
and brush over the top and the sides with the glaze.

Beetroot and Cabbage Salad

Finely shred a head of cabbage and put into salt water for an
hour to make it crisp. Then drain it, dry it in a cloth and put
into a salad bowl and add to it the following:—

A cup of finely shredded celery, two finely chopped onions,
two finely chopped green peppers and a cup of mayonnaise
to which has been added a spoonful and a half of salt and a
teaspoonful of paprika. Before adding the mayonnaise add a
large cup of chopped beetroot.

Brandied Peaches

Put half a cup of water into a preserving pan and then in
alternate layers, peaches and sugar, scalding and skinning
the peaches first and allowing half a pound of loaf sugar to
each pound of peaches. Allow them to boil slowly (stirring
occasionally) until the sugar is dissolved. Then remove from
the fire and leave them in a covered earthenware jar for two
days. Then carefully turn them back into the preserving pan
and let them boil till clear. Ladle out the peaches and let the
syrup boil a few minutes longer; then strain it and leave it to
cool.

Take half as much brandy as syrup and mix it with the syrup. Fill the jars with the peaches and pour the syrup over them till the jar is full, then screw on the lids.

Menu 16

Hot Potato Soup

Peel and boil three large potatoes till soft, put them through a sieve. Cook a tablespoonful of onion in a pint of milk till soft, then add to it pepper and salt and the potatoes. Let them boil, pass through a sieve, then stir in two tablespoonfuls of butter, a level tablespoonful of flour and bring again to the boil, stirring all the time. Add four tablespoonfuls of whipped cream and put boiling hot into the thermos.

Marinade of Halibut

Cook some halibut and, when cool, skin and bone it. Arrange it in nice pieces at the bottom of a salad bowl. Then slice as thinly as possible some onions and pimentos and put a layer of them over the fish together with two cloves, a bay leaf, cayenne and black pepper and salt, and add a few drops of olive oil. Repeat these layers of fish and seasoning till the fish is used up and pour over the whole a glass of white wine or white wine vinegar. Leave it for several hours.

Cucumber and Gherkin Salad

Peel and slice thinly a small cucumber, cover it with salt and put it on one side for an hour. Then take some gherkins and chop them.

Drain the cucumber and dry it in a cloth. Put a layer at the bottom of the salad bowl and then a layer of gherkin, and so on, and leave a few whole gherkins to decorate it with.

Pour over the salad a dressing of oil, vinegar, pepper, salt and mustard.

Menu 17

Lobster Cream

Mince the meat of a lobster and mix it with half a teacupful of breadcrumbs and half a pint of cream. Beat up two eggs and add them and season with salt, cayenne and ordinary pepper.

Put the mixture into a buttered soufflé dish, tie a buttered paper over and steam in a bainmarie for forty-five minutes. Turn out and serve on lettuce leaves and decorate with the claws of the lobster.

Pigeon Pie

Line the bottom of a pie dish with small collops of lean beef rump steak that has been previously fried in butter. On this, place the halves of three or four pigeons also previously fried. Season with chopped mushrooms, parsley, shallot, pepper and salt.

Pour half a pint of sauce, gravy or water with a little mush-room catsup in the pan the meat has been fried in to detach the glaze, and pour this over the pigeons. Add the hard-boiled yolks and white of three or four eggs, cut in slices;

cover with puff pastry, and bake the pie in a moderate oven for about an hour and a quarter.

Orange and Celery Salad

Slice the oranges and chop up the celery. Make a dressing of the juice that comes away from the oranges while they are being sliced, mixed with pepper, salt, oil and vinegar, and pour over the salad, using the top part of the celery and watercress to decorate it.

Menu 18

An Excellent Fish Pie

Take a pound of cod or any good white fish and cut it up.

Then slice an onion and put it into a pan with an ounce of butter to brown.

Add the fish, pepper, salt and seasoning and shake it over the fire for a few minutes. Then pour in a pint of hot water; bring it to the boil and then skim it carefully.

Add a cupful of cold semi-boiled Patna rice and cook the whole till the rice is done and the liquid absorbed.

Melt an ounce of butter in another pan, let it brown slightly, mix in a teaspoonful of curry powder and add this to the cooked fish and rice and mix all together. Season it well.

In the meantime line a pie dish with short crust, put in the mixture, make a lid of pastry and bake in a moderate oven for about an hour.

Serve cold.

Egg, Watercress and Nut Salad

Hard boil two eggs. Divide the watercress into sprigs, lay them in the bowl with hard-boiled eggs cut in slices mixed with it and arranged in a ring round the bowl. Chop or mince any kind of nut and sprinkle over the salad.

Dress with oil and vinegar.

Grapefruit Salad with Kirsch

Peel the grapefruit, and take off all the white skin underneath the peel.

Cut into thin cubes, removing all the hard part and pips, and putting them into a jug to which half a pint of cold water is added, and the juice.

Arrange the grapefruit in a bowl.

Strain the water with the pips and core, add enough sugar to make into a thin syrup and flavour it with three tablespoonfuls of Kirsch. Pour over the salad.

Menu 19

Game Terrine

Put some raw joints of boned game into a glass soufflé dish and season very heavily with black pepper, cayenne and salt. Fill up the dish with consommé and bake in the oven. Serve cold.

Marcel Boulestin—*Conduct of the Kitchen.*

Consommé

Put a piece of beef, a few bones and a marrow bone in salted water. Bring to the boil and skim well, then add two onions, two or three carrots, one turnip, one leek, parsley, one clove and a little pepper. Let it simmer for at least six hours. Skim well, leaving no fat. Strain.

MARCEL BOULESTIN.

Horseradish Sauce

Beat half a cupful of butter to a cream and gradually beat into it two ounces of freshly grated horseradish; then add a tablespoonful of lemon juice and pass through a sieve.

Spiced Beetroot

8 small beetroots, 1 pound of brown sugar, 1 pint of vinegar, 1 dessertspoonful of whole cloves, ½ ounce of cinnamon stick.

Choose small beets of equal size, wash them well and cook till tender, not allowing them to bleed. Drain them and remove the ends. Boil the vinegar and sugar together with the spice for twenty minutes, add the beetroots cut in four lengthways and heat them to boiling point. Put into wide mouthed bottles and cork tightly.

Potatoes in Jackets

See page 49.

Menu 20

*Purée of Smoked Haddock with
Tartare Sauce*

Scrape away the flesh from one or more cooked smoked haddocks and make into a purée by pressing through a sieve. Mix it with a well-beaten egg.

Arrange in a pile at the bottom of a dish and cover it with a sauce tartare. Garnish with slices of cold hard-boiled egg and sprigs of watercress.

Sauce Tartare

See page 40.

Chicken and Bread Sauce

Cook a chicken in the ordinary way. Divide it into tidy pieces and arrange it on a dish with watercress.

Serve with it cold bread sauce.

Bread Sauce

The secret of making good bread sauce is to flavour the milk before adding it to the bread. The breadcrumbs should be stale, dried in the oven and then pounded.

First boil a small onion for five minutes; then put half a pint of milk into a saucepan and add to it the boiled onion cut into pieces, a dozen peppercorns, not quite a teaspoonful of salt, and either a good pinch of nutmeg or a leaf of mace, or half a dozen cloves. Watch the milk to see that it does not boil and let it simmer over a gentle fire until it has time to absorb the various flavourings. Every time it begins to bubble move it from the fire to cool down a little. As this process reduces the milk a little more must be added.

The Gentle Art of Cookery.

Chinese Orange Salad

Peel and cut the oranges into slices lengthways, steep some shelled walnuts in vinegar, drain them and add to the oranges, and pour over the salad a dressing made of oil, lemon juice and ginger seasoned with salt and pepper.

Chocolate Soufflé

Beat to a cream two ounces of castor sugar and one and a half ounces of butter, add three tablespoonfuls of grated unsweetened chocolate, the yolks of two eggs and five tablespoonfuls of breadcrumbs. Mix well and pour into a mould to set. No cooking is required.

Turn out the next day and serve with Devonshire cream.

Menu 21

Hot Green Pea Soup

Take a quart of stock or water and add a pint of shelled peas, the pea shells broken up, a few leaves of spinach and lettuce, a pinch of sugar, salt and pepper, and a handful of mint.

Boil until the spinach and lettuce are soft and pass them through a hair sieve, but remove the pods of the peas.

Meanwhile cook the peas themselves in two ounces of butter, a gill of boiling water, a little salt and sugar, shaking frequently till soft.

Pass them through a sieve and add to the rest of the soup. Bring the whole to the boil, flavour, thicken with a little arrowroot and keep some of the peas whole to add to the soup before it is served.

Pour boiling hot into a thermos.

Salad of Curried Rice, Olives and Cucumber

Prepare some cold cooked Patna rice and arrange it in a ring round the salad bowl; then chop some olives and thinly slice a small cucumber. Arrange a ring of each inside the ring of rice and pour over the cucumber and olives the following sauce:

Beat up together half a cup of sour cream, three table-spoonfuls of Chili sauce, two tablespoonfuls of tomato ketchup, the juice of half a lemon, half a teaspoonful of red pepper and pepper and salt to taste. Beat till thick and pour over the salad.

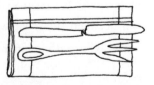

Menu 22

Eggs with Anchovy Butter

Hard boil as many eggs as are required. Cut them in half. Remove the yolks and mix them with a little anchovy sauce, butter, pepper and chopped parsley. Fill the halves with the mixture and put each half on a small square of fried bread which has been spread with butter and anchovy paste. Serve on a bed of watercress.

Cold Rabbit Pie

Take two young rabbits, wash them thoroughly, joint and bone them and put the pieces in salted water for an hour or so.

Then put them into a saucepan with just enough water to cover them. Add two shallots, a bay leaf, thyme, parsley and sage, and pepper and salt. Let it simmer very gently for about two hours. Half fry some rashers of bacon and cover them thickly with a mixture of minced onion and parsley. Then roll up the slices of bacon and fill the pie dish with the rabbit and the bacon placed in between the meat with slices of hard-boiled egg. Season heavily with pepper, salt and cayenne and fill up with good stock to which a teaspoonful of Lea & Perrin's Worcester sauce and a teaspoonful of Harvey's sauce can be added. Put on a pie crust according to the directions on page 24.

Cold Catsup

Chop very fine a quarter of a peck of ripe tomatoes after peeling them and removing the seeds, three-quarters of a quart of celery, a pint of onions and two apples. Drain them overnight and add next day:

1 root of horseradish grated, ¼ cup of salt, ¼ cup of white mustard seed, ¾ cup of brown sugar, ½ teaspoonful of powdered cloves, ½ teaspoonful of powdered mace, ¼ teaspoonful of cayenne, 1 teaspoonful of cinnamon, ¾ quart of vinegar.

Mix all together without cooking, and bottle.

Watercress Salad

Cut four or five strips of bacon into dice and brown them in a pan. When cooked draw off all the fat except about four tablespoonfuls.

Put into a basin one-half teaspoonful of sugar and the same of mustard and paprika, one teaspoonful of salt and four tablespoonfuls of wine vinegar. Pour this into the fat left in the pan and add the cooked bacon. Prepare the watercress, put it in the salad bowl and pour over it the bacon and dressing.

Decorate with hard-boiled egg.

Menu 23

Cold Roast Duck and Apple Sauce

Cook the duck in the ordinary way and cut into tidy pieces, leaving the brown skin.

Decorate with grated horseradish and watercress.

Apple Sauce

Peel, core and slice good cooking apples and put into a sauce-pan with a tablespoonful of water and let them simmer till soft; drain and stir in a little butter and sugar.

Green Pea, Orange and Beetroot Salad

Cut rather thick slices of beetroot and then cut them into dice. Peel and cut the oranges, removing all the white skin and hard pieces and cut into dice also. Then take half a pint of cooked green peas. Mix together, season with pepper and salt and pour over the following dressing:

Beat together the yolks of two eggs, a tablespoonful of lemon juice, a tablespoonful of tarragon vinegar, pepper, salt and enough oil to thicken, adding it drop by drop.

Menu 24

Cold Consommé

See page 59.

Unless consommé can be made with great care it is better to buy it already made. The whole art of making a good consommé depends upon the slowness with which it is boiled and the amount of skimming that it gets.

Take four pounds of brisket of beef and about twice the amount of cold salted water and bring it very slowly to the boil, never really letting it go off the boil but never letting it do more than simmer. The skimming must be constant, for this can never be successfully done afterwards. When the skimming has been thoroughly done, add two onions stuck with cloves, two carrots, two leeks, two turnips, a tomato, a little celery, pepper and salt and a bouquet of herbs. Then let it simmer in the same way for another five or six hours.

Then strain and remove the fat.

It should be put in the refrigerator for some hours before it is put into the thermos, because it must be served very cold.

Chicken and Bread Sauce

See page 61

Watercress, Beetroot and Nasturtium Salad

Slice the beetroot very thin, and divide the watercress into sprigs.

Take young nasturtium leaves and arrange the salad in the bowl with walls of each, placing the beetroot in between the two greens. Decorate with nasturtium flowers, and pour over the salad a dressing made of nasturtium seeds, oil, vinegar, salt and pepper.

Torone and Quince Jam

Torone is the Spanish nougat which is made in many varieties, either soft or hard. It can be bought from the Spanish restaurant or from Fortnum & Mason.

Any good quince jam can be used.

The torone and the quince jam are served in slices and are eaten together.

Menu 25

Sausages and French Mustard

See page 36.

Beetroot and Gherkin Salad

Some of the gherkins are left whole and the others are chopped. Only the tiny gherkins are used. The beetroot is cut into inch cubes and also into thin round slices. The cubes are mixed with the chopped gherkins and the slices of beetroot are used for decoration with the whole gherkins. Over the whole pour the following sauce:

The yolks of 2 eggs, 1 tablespoonful of lemon juice, 1 tablespoonful of tarragon vinegar, enough olive oil to thicken.

Add a dessertspoonful of Chili sauce and half a teaspoonful of Escoffier's sauce "Diable", salt, pepper and paprika.

Apple Flan

Mix together two ounces of butter and two tablespoonfuls of castor sugar; add the juice of half a lemon, the very thin rind of half a lemon, a teaspoonful of mixed spice and an egg beaten up with a cupful of milk. Mix well and add a pound of thinly sliced juicy apples. Leave it for two hours, and line a plate or sandwich tin with puff pastry. Fill with the mixture after removing the lemon rind.

Slice and blanche some Jordan almonds and decorate the top of the flan with them.

Bake in a hot oven for about twenty minutes.

Menu 26

Mousse of Chicken Liver

Rub two or three chicken livers through a sieve. Then put into a saucepan a quarter of a pound of butter and, when melted, stir into it three tablespoonfuls of flour. Add some tepid stock little by little and mix well, stirring all the time till it thickens, and draw away from the fire when the sauce is thick enough for a spoon to stand up in. Then add by degrees the yolks of three eggs to the chicken livers, season well with pepper and salt, add the sauce and, last of all, the stiffly beaten whites. Pour into a buttered mould which has been rubbed with garlic and cook in a bain-marie for thirty minutes, then put the mould into the oven for about ten minutes in a dish of water. Turn it out and serve cold.

Caraway Straws

Put into a bowl five ounces of butter and enough flour to make into a dough, add a little water and a good pinch of salt.

Work to a stiff dough and then roll out on a floured board and cut into lengths like cheese straws. Brush over with yolk of egg, sprinkle with salt and caraway seeds and bake in a moderate oven till brown.

Cumberland Sauce

Mix all together a stick of grated horseradish, two ounces of red currant jelly, a tablespoonful of mixed mustard, the grated rind and juice of two lemons and two oranges, and a tablespoonful of vinegar.

Spaghetti and Green Pepper Salad

Cook the spaghetti in the usual way in a large pan of boiling salted water. Drain it and chop it slightly.

Red or green pimentos can be used, or both. They should be chopped rather finely, and if the skin is too hard they could be baked in the oven first. The spaghetti and the chopped peppers should be mixed together in the salad bowl, seasoned with salt and covered with a dressing of oil, vinegar, chopped parsley and onion and sprinkled with powdered nuts.

Menu 27

Crab Tartlets

Make some pastry as on page 24. Line some tartlets with it and bake them in the oven. When cold fill them with fresh crab meat to which a little lemon juice has been added.

Macédoine of Vegetables

Cut into dice cold cooked potatoes, beetroot, carrots, turnips, mushrooms, cauliflower, artichoke, cucumber, celery and any vegetables that are available. Toss them lightly together in a bowl, but put the beetroots on one side or they will spoil the appearance of the others.

Marinate them in a tablespoonful of oil well mixed with two tablespoonfuls of lemon juice, two saltspoonfuls of salt, one saltspoonful of paprika and two tablespoonfuls of grated onion. Marinate the beetroot separately.

Cover the bowl and put it in the refrigerator. When ready to serve drain well, add the beetroots, and pile them in a salad dish on a bed of mustard and cress surrounded by a border of tomatoes, alternating with pickled onions, pickled walnuts and olives. Cut thin strips of pimento and arrange them in criss-cross fashion on the top after a thick mayonnaise has been poured over the vegetables in the middle of the dish.

Strips of boned anchovies can also be used to decorate the top.

Pickled Peaches

Wipe the peaches and stick them with two or three cloves in each.

Boil together a quart of vinegar with two pounds of loaf sugar, skim and then add a quarter of an ounce of cinnamon bark. Place enough peaches in the syrup to just come up to the surface of the syrup, then let them boil till spongy but not till soft.

Take out with a skimmer and place the peaches in glass jars as they are cooked. Strain the syrup. Let it cool slightly and pour it over the peaches. Screw down the jars when cool.

Green Butter

Well wash and bone two ounces of anchovies. Boil a large handful of very green parsley and, when tender, chop it fine. Leave the lid off while boiling and put it immediately under the cold tap when boiled.

Beat together the anchovies, the parsley and four ounces of fresh butter, make into a paste and pot.

Menu 28

Asparagus Soup

Take a bundle of asparagus, half a peck of spinach, a large handful of parsley and the same of spring onions. Wash them well. Drain them and boil them in two quarts of water, with a piece of butter and some salt. As soon as the asparagus is cooked, drain off the liquor and keep it. Pound the asparagus in a mortar and add it to the liquor. Reheat and add two ounces of flour mixed with the same quantity of butter, pepper, salt and a spoonful of white sugar. Stir till it thickens without allowing it to boil. Then put in the refrigerator, make very cold and pour into a thermos.

Salmon Loaf

Remove the skin and bones from a pound of cooked salmon, break it with a fork; add two well-beaten eggs, a cup of white breadcrumbs soaked in milk, a tablespoonful of lemon juice and salt and pepper to taste.

Pack the fish into a covered mould which has been well buttered and steam for an hour in a bain-marie. Turn out and serve either whole or cut into slices. Decorate with thin slices of lemon and parsley.

This can also be made with tinned salmon.

Spinach Soufflé

Cook enough spinach to make ten ounces of purée.

Melt together a tablespoonful each of flour and butter and, when a smooth paste, add a teaspoonful of finely chopped onion. Cook for a few minutes and then add half a pint of spinach purée. Let the mixture cool till most of the moisture is absorbed. Pour into a basin and stir in the yolks of three eggs which have been mixed with a gill of cream and strained. Season well with plenty of black pepper and salt and then add the stiffly beaten whites of the eggs.

Butter a soufflé mould, fill it with the mixture and bake in a pan of water in a moderate oven for about twenty minutes.

Menu 29

Foie Gras Tartlets

Make some pastry as on page 24. Line some small tins with it and bake them in the oven. When cold fill them with pâté de foie gras. If the Strasbourg foie gras is too expensive the Hungarian can be used and it is excellent in flavour, or the tartlets can be filled with the home-made chicken's liver as on page 26.

Horseradish Sauce

See page 59.

Sweet Potatoes in their Jackets

See page 49.

Menu 30

Cold Curry and Rice

Cut one or two pounds of lean mutton into dice and fry lightly in butter. Lift this on to a plate and fry in the same pan two onions and a sour apple cut in slices.

When golden brown, add a large spoonful of curry powder and fry for another minute. Add a small spoonful of flour, then mix in the mutton and add half a pint of stock or gravy, a large spoonful of chutney, the juice of one lemon and one orange, one spoonful of desiccated coconut and a quarter of a chive of garlic. Let it simmer slowly for two hours, adding more gravy if it gets too dry.

Put in a cool place and serve very cold, surrounded by a wall of cold Patna rice and sprinkled with grated horseradish.

Rice for the Curry

Take a large pan of cold water, put a handful of salt in it and, when it boils, throw in about two ounces or more of unpolished Patna rice. Let it boil very quickly for ten minutes or more, then pour it quickly into an enamelled colander, put it under the cold water tap and leave it for a few moments in the colander over a saucepan of water to drain. Then flick it with a fork, gather it into a clean cloth and put it into the oven for a few minutes to dry. Each grain must be separate.

Tomato, Coconut and Olive Salad

Skin the tomatoes after scalding them and cut them in slices, making a thick bed of them at the bottom of the salad bowl. Then chop two good handfuls of olives after stoning them, and sprinkle over grated coconut. Pour over the salad the following dressing:

Bake a pound of tomatoes in a covered jar till soft. Strain through a sieve, and to every eight ounces of pulp add four ounces of brown sugar and a quarter of a pint of vinegar. Boil for twenty minutes and, when cold, add ¼ ounce of mustard seed, ¼ ounce of salt, ¼ ounce of ground ginger, ¼ ounce of cayenne pepper.

Stir well and pour over the salad.

The sauce is better made a week beforehand and will keep for months if properly cooked.

Lemon Pie

Line a dish with short pastry and, when baked, fill it with the following mixture:

Take a tablespoonful of cornflour, the yolks of two eggs, a cupful of water and mix into a smooth paste. Add the juice of a lemon and the grated rind of half a lemon, half a cupful of sugar and a piece of butter the size of a walnut. Boil in a double saucepan till thick, and when cold put into the pastry. Beat the whites of the eggs with four tablespoonfuls of white sugar, and pile on the top, putting into the oven for a few minutes to brown.

Menu 31

Hot Carrot Soup

Cook two cups of coarsely grated carrots till tender and pass through a sieve. Boil half a cup of Patna rice till soft in a double saucepan with two cups of milk.

Brown two slices of onion in a pan with two ounces of butter and a sprig of parsley, and stir in two level tablespoonfuls of flour and season well with salt and black pepper.

Mix the carrots with the rice and milk, and pour slowly into the flour and butter.

Boil for a few minutes and strain.

Jamaica Mould

Mince a pound of veal, toss it in two ounces of butter; add a Spanish onion chopped fine, pepper, salt, two tablespoonfuls of tomato sauce and a teaspoonful of curry powder, half a pint of stock, and two ounces of rice. Let them all simmer till cooked and the stock is absorbed. Mix well, fill a buttered mould and press it down with a weight on the top. Turn it out next day and serve cold with a savoury grapefruit salad.

Savoury Grapefruit Salad

Peel and slice the grapefruit as for a sweet salad but season with cayenne, black pepper and salt.

Menu 32

Cold Prawn Patties

Shell as many prawns as are required and leave them to marinate in a bowl with a wineglassful of sherry and a table-spoonful of lemon juice.

Line some patty pans with good puff pastry and fill them with the prawns, some chopped olives, a little essence of anchovy and the liquid in which they marinated. Cover with paste and bake in a quick oven. Leave to get cold and serve.

Beef Salad

Cut some thin slices from a cold sirloin of beef and spread them with this mixture.

Take a handful of finely chopped olives, two anchovies,

four gherkins, the hard-boiled yolks of two eggs and a little chutney all mixed together.

Then sprinkle over the top some grated horseradish, and arrange the slices in a long dish on a bed of lettuce leaves with rolls of very thin cooked ham, cold fried baby sausages, cold chip potatoes, a bunch of watercress and green tomato chutney.

Asparagus Soufflé

Take a very large bundle of asparagus. Cook it in the usual way; drain it and chop off all the heads as far as they are tender. Put them through a sieve.

Then take half a pint of milk and a quarter of a pint of cream, beat them together and add six leaves of gelatine dissolved in a little water.

Stir in the asparagus, season with pepper, salt and cayenne, and pour into a soufflé dish and leave to set. Turn out the next day or when firm, and decorate with cucumber.

Menu 33

Marinated Herrings

If possible choose herrings with soft roes. Put into a pan a sliced carrot, a sliced onion, a clove of garlic, a bouquet of herbs, salt and peppercorns which have been bruised. Then add a pint of good white wine and two tablespoonfuls of vinegar and a pint of water. Bring to the boil and let them simmer for five minutes longer. Leave the fish in the liquid till cold and then serve in a fireproof dish with some of the liquid to which has been added small pickled onions and gherkins.

Knap Pie

Take two pounds of knuckle of veal and let it simmer in a saucepan covered with water for several hours. Then put it on one side to cool.

Cut it in slices when cold, and also cut some thin slices of cold boiled beef and some hard-boiled eggs.

Proceed to fill up the pie dish with alternate layers of veal, beef and egg. Season well and pour over it as much of the liquor the veal was boiled in as will fill the dish. Put a good pastry on the top and serve cold.

Menu 34

Hot Consommé

See same recipe as for Cold Consommé on page 59 and serve with pirogs or herb pasties.

Pirogs are eaten in Russia with soup and can be filled with meat, ham, fish or cheese, but they are usually stuffed with herbs and are not unlike the herby pastes that were so much in vogue in England in the eighteenth century.

Paste for Pirogs

Dissolve an ounce of yeast in ten ounces of warm milk and stir in a pound of flour and leave it to rise in a warm place.

Then add a little salt, a quarter of a pound of butter, two eggs and enough flour to make a firm paste. Knead it well till it no longer sticks to the fingers, roll out to about half an inch in thickness, cut into rounds or crescents and leave to rise again. Then place the mixture on it. Cover with another one and pinch the edges, and bake.

Cook's Tour of European Kitchens.

Stuffing for Pirogs

1. Cooked mushrooms and hard-boiled egg chopped fine and mixed with cooked Patna rice; *or*

2. Boiled cabbage mixed with butter, mushrooms and hard-boiled egg; *or*

3. Parsley, shallots, spinach and hard-boiled egg chopped small.

Pressed Veal

Get a breast of veal boned and boil it in a cloth tied up very tightly with half a pound of sausage meat and three hard-boiled eggs for three hours.

Leave it all night under heavy weights, and glaze it before serving.

Serve with it the following sauce:

Cut into shreds a few slices of cucumber, two pickled gherkins, a hard-boiled egg, a dozen blanched almonds and a dozen pistachio nuts, a teaspoonful of chopped parsley, a small quantity of chives or onions, a little chopped tarragon and one or two truffles. Add two tablespoonfuls of olive oil, one tablespoonful of vinegar, one dessertspoonful of tarragon vinegar, salt and pepper.

Mousse of Vegetables

Mix two cupfuls of finely cut celery with the thinly grated rind of an orange and a dozen chopped walnuts.

Mix with a stiff mayonnaise made without mustard and serve in the shells of lemons or oranges on a bed of lettuce. The pulp of the oranges or lemons can be added if liked.

Menu 35

Salmon Served in Lemons

Halve the lemons; scoop out the inside. Take the remains of some cold salmon and work it into a paste with butter, salt, pepper, lemon juice and cream.

Serve the lemons on a bed of mustard and cress.

Partridge Pie

Truss, loose, singe and divide into halves three young partridges. Season and fry them in butter. Line the pie dish with thin collops of veal and half-boiled bacon; season with chopped mushrooms, and parsley, pepper and salt; pour a gill of onion sauce over the veal; then place neatly the halves of partridges, repeating the seasoning and the onion sauce; add some hard-boiled yolks of eggs, cover with paste; bake for about an hour and a quarter, and pour in some good gravy before serving.

Galantine of Vegetables

Cook three ounces of macaroni and separately four ounces of lentils with an onion, a bay leaf and a bouquet of thyme. Drain them well.

Then soak five ounces of breadcrumbs in water, and chop finely two tablespoonfuls of stoned black olives and a hard-boiled egg. Chop an onion small and fry it in two ounces of butter and gradually add the macaroni, lentils, breadcrumbs from which the water has been thoroughly squeezed, the olives, and egg and an egg beaten up. Mix well together, butter a mould, pour the mixture in, and cover it with greased paper and bake in a moderate oven for two hours. Leave in the mould till it is ready to be served.

Anchovy Biscuits

Knead two ounces of flour on a pastry board with two ounces of butter.

Season with cayenne pepper, salt, and put enough anchovy sauce to give them a distinct flavour of anchovy.

Roll out to a thickness of an eighth of an inch and cut into straws a quarter of an inch thick.

Bake for about three minutes.

Menu 36

Hot Onion Soup

Slice four large onions and fry in butter till a golden brown.

Put them into a casserole with a quart of stock and season well with pepper, salt and herbs and let them simmer for half an hour. Then add a cup of cream and an egg beaten with it. Stir until smooth without letting it boil and put straight into the thermos. Serve with grated parmesan floating on the top.

Chicken and Leek Pie

Boil a chicken in a quarter of a pint of cold water to each pound weight of the chicken and let it simmer for two hours. Pour away the liquid, and put it on one side. Cut up the chicken, flavour the broth with salt, onion, pepper, etc. Scald some leeks by pouring boiling water over them, split them and cut them into pieces about an inch long.

Lay the chicken in a pie dish with slices of cold tongue, the leeks and the broth, and some finely chopped parsley. Cover it with a short crust and bake.

When baked take off the top ornament of pastry and pour in three tablespoonfuls of cream heated over hot water and then replace the ornament.

Ham, Beetroot and Pea Salad

Slice and chop the beetroots into dice, and also the ham. Cook the peas and mix all together and pour over the following dressing:

Mix together a grated stick of horseradish, two ounces of

red currant jelly, a tablespoonful of mixed mustard and the grated rind and juice of two lemons and two oranges, and a tablespoonful of vinegar.

Menu 37

Shrimp Pie

Butter a pie dish; plunge six large tomatoes into boiling water, skin them and put them through a sieve. Put a layer of crumbs at the bottom of the pie dish, then a layer of tomatoes, with a tiny pinch of castor sugar sprinkled over them. Then put in a pint of shelled shrimps and season them. Cover with more crumbs and put some small pieces of butter on top. Bake very slowly for half an hour and serve cold.

If preferred this dish can have a pastry cover.

Beetroot and Apple Salad Purée

Peel and cut into slices two beetroots and four sour apples. Put them into a saucepan with a finely chopped onion and two ounces of butter.

Season with salt, pepper and a good deal of nutmeg and let it simmer till reduced to a smooth pulp.

Serve cold.

Treacle Tart

Warm some treacle and stir in enough breadcrumbs to thicken it and add the juice of a lemon and some of the thin rind. Put a layer of pastry on a plate and fill it with the mixture and bake; a lid of pastry can be put over the treacle if wished. Bake for about thirty to forty-five minutes.

Menu 38

Anchovy Tartines

Make some toast, cut into rounds and butter liberally each round. Then place on each a stoned olive and curl round the olive an anchovy. Chop some hard-boiled eggs and sprinkle over the whole.

Ham Loaves

Cook some potatoes in their skins and mash half a pound of the potato with half a pound of grated lean ham and a quarter of a pound of breadcrumbs.

Add plenty of pepper and salt, the thin rind of half a lemon, an ounce of butter and two lightly beaten eggs and some grated nutmeg and chopped parsley.

Make into small loaves. Brush them over with beaten egg and bake.

Serve cold with spiced prunes. See page 122.

Tarragon, Chervil and Lettuce Salad

Take the outer leaves from a lettuce and tear the inner part to pieces (do not chop it); mix it with some tarragon and chervil treated in the same way and pour over it the following sauce:

A grated stick of horseradish, 2 ounces of red currant jelly, 1 tablespoonful of mixed mustard, 1 tablespoonful of vinegar, the grated rind and juice of a lemon and an orange.

Mix together and pour over the salad.

Menu 39

Crab Soufflé

Remove all the flesh from a boiled crab, leaving out one claw. Season the flesh well with salt, pepper, a cupful of mayonnaise and a cupful of liquid aspic jelly. Add four leaves of gelatine dissolved in a little water and stir into the mixture. Put half of this into a soufflé dish, then half the flesh from the claw that has been reserved, then the rest of the mixture, and then the rest of the claw. When cold, turn out on to a bed of lettuce.

Pheasant with Tartare Sauce

See for Tartare Sauce, page 40.

Lettuce and Cucumber Salad

See page 38.

Coffee Soufflé

Make three-quarters of a pint of strong coffee and add to it a quarter of a pint of milk. Put it into a double saucepan with two ounces of sugar and half an ounce of gelatine dissolved in a little hot water.

Beat up the yolks of three eggs and whip them with two ounces of sugar; add a pinch of salt and put this into the coffee and stir till it thickens. Then add the stiffly beaten whites, but take it off the fire before doing this. Flavour with vanilla, pour into a wetted mould and leave till set. Serve covered with whipped cream.

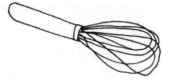

Menu 40

Eggs Stuffed with Sardines

Hard boil some eggs. Cut them in half, remove the yolk. Take one or two small Norwegian sardines, bone them, and pound them in a mortar with the yolk of the eggs, a little milk and cream and seasoning, pepper and salt. Fill the eggs with these, serve them on toast surrounded by mustard and cress.

Dutch Roll and Orange Salad

1 pound of lean mutton, 2 tablespoonfuls of breadcrumbs, 1 dessertspoonful of chutney, 1 egg, ¼ teaspoonful of jamaica pepper, salt.

Mince the mutton twice, add the breadcrumbs, chutney and seasoning, and mix well. Then beat the egg well and add it and form the mixture into a roll. Sprinkle it with flour and bake it on a baking dish for an hour, basting it from time to time.

Serve with piquante sauce and orange salad.

Piquante Sauce

Chop two shallots and put into a pan with a bouquet of herbs and three tablespoonfuls of vinegar. Reduce to a third and add some stock. Mix with a little flour and butter, season and add chopped gherkins, capers, parsley and fresh-ground black pepper.

Pears in Brandy

Use half a pound of sugar to every pound of pears. Put half a cup of water into a preserving pan, then the peeled pears and sugar in alternate layers; boil, stirring occasionally at first until the sugar is dissolved.

Let it stand in covered earthenware jar for two days, then turn carefully into preserving pan and boil till clear. Skim the pears out and let syrup boil a few minutes longer. Then strain and let it cool.

Take half as much brandy as you have syrup and pour over the pears when in the jars.

Menu 41

Hot Tomato Soup

Boil a pound of tomatoes till soft and then put them through a sieve.

Boil a pint of milk with an ounce of chopped onion. Put an ounce of butter into a pan and stir in a good dessertspoonful of cornflour till smooth, then remove the onion from the milk and add the milk to the paste, season well with salt and pepper and, when boiling, add the sieved tomatoes. Stir well together and add a little cream before serving.

Veal with Tunny Fish and Anchovies

This is a famous Milanese dish.

Remove all fat and gristle from two pounds of filleted veal, then take two anchovies, cut them into eight thin strips and lard the veal with them and tie up the fillet with string. Put into a saucepan enough cold water to cover the veal, add an onion stuck with two cloves, two sliced carrots, a chopped stick of celery, a bay leaf, salt and pepper to taste. Bring this to the boil and then add the veal and let it simmer for an hour and a half. Then remove the meat and let it drain.

Carve it into very thin slices and put them into a casserole, closely packed, and cover with the following sauce:

Bone two anchovies and pound them in a mortar with four ounces of tunny fish in oil.

Then add olive oil gradually as in making a mayonnaise, and last of all the juice of a large lemon. Enough sauce is needed to cover the meat; then add two tablespoonfuls of capers and let it stand in a cold place for a day or so.

The dish should be decorated with slices of lemon.

Egg Pie

Cut three hard-boiled eggs into slices and lay them in a pie dish, sprinkle them with salt and pepper and the following mixture: 1 teaspoonful of minced onion, 2 teaspoonfuls of chopped parsley, 1 tablespoonful of grated cheese.

Pour round some white béchamel sauce, cover with mashed potatoes and bake in a brisk oven.

Menu 42

Crab Ravigote

Take a pound of cooked crab meat. Soak it in vinegar for a few minutes and then drain.

Make a thick mayonnaise in the usual way with yolk of egg, oil and vinegar, and season it. Add a teaspoonful of chopped parsley and a tablespoonful of chopped gherkins. Mix all together and add the crab meat.

Fill the shells, cover with mayonnaise and decorate with strips of red and green pimentos.

Fricandeau of Veal

Take a slice about an inch and a half thick from a cushion of veal and cut it with the grain of the meat.

Beat it well and lard it carefully on the cut side. Then braise it with stock on a bed of sliced and fried carrots and onions in the proportion of an ounce of each to a pound of meat, a bouquet of parsley, some thyme, a bay leaf, a clove of garlic and an ounce and a half of blanched rind of bacon.

Cook as slowly as possible till the meat can be pricked without exuding blood and until it can be cut with a spoon.

Then dish it very carefully, strain the liquor and pour over it and leave it to get cold.

The veal can be glazed if liked, and the thick jelly which surrounds it should be decorated with mounds of cold peas, cold chopped carrot, celery and beetroot.

AMBROSE HEATH in *Good Food*.

Grapefruit and Walnut Salad

Shell the walnuts, and peel and slice the grapefruit. Mix together and pour over a dressing of oil and lemon juice seasoned with salt and pepper.

Charlotte Russe with Strawberries

Trim about six ounces of sponge rusks so as to make them fit closely to one another, and line the bottom and sides of a mould with them, and fill it with the following mixture:

Pick the stalks from a pound of strawberries, bruise them

with a wooden spoon with six ounces of sifted sugar, rub this mixture through a hair sieve, add a pint of whipped cream and two ounces of clarified isinglass. Mix and fill the mould with it.

Any fruit that is in season can be used, or plain whipped cream mixed with isinglass and flavoured with vanilla or jam.

Menu 43

Quiche Lorraine

Line a flan ring with light puff pastry and bake.

When cooked, but not coloured, cover the bottom with some slices of cooked ham. Make a custard with three yolks and one white of egg, half a pint of cream and pepper and salt. Put into the flan and bake till custard is set.

Tomato and Cucumber Salad

Peel the tomatoes and the cucumber; slice the cucumber very thin and the tomatoes as thin as possible without breaking them.

Arrange them in a salad bowl in alternate layers. Sprinkle with finely chopped hard-boiled egg, and pour over the following dressing:

Mix together a teaspoonful of salt, a quarter of a teaspoonful of paprika, one tablespoonful of horseradish, two tablespoonfuls of Chili sauce, one tablespoonful of lemon juice and six tablespoonfuls of olive oil.

Menu 44

Mousse of Chicken

Take a cooked chicken, bone it and skin it and cut the meat into dice. Pound it to a paste and season it well with pepper, salt, cayenne and a little spice. Then stir into it the whites of two eggs; after beating it well, put it through a sieve and stir into it by degrees half a pint of cream. Cook in a bain-marie or in the oven and, when cold, sprinkle with finely chopped parsley.

Pork Chops with Apple Purée

Remove all the fat from the chops and cut the bones very short; then boil them with a pair of pork trotters, each cut into four, in three parts of water to one of white wine. Skim well while boiling. Add pepper, salt, cloves, bay leaves and the thin peel of a lemon. When the meat is cooked take it out and drain it and place it in a deep dish.

Strain the stock and reduce it and, when lukewarm, pour it over the meat and stand the dish in a cold place.

Serve cold with an apple purée.

Beetroot, Horseradish and Celery Salad

Take a head of celery and chop it into small pieces. Shred a stick of horseradish and mix it with the celery. Chop into dice two small beetroots and add them last of all. Cover with grated horseradish. Pour over the salad the following sauce:

Stir two beaten eggs with three tablespoonfuls of milk and the same of vinegar in a double saucepan. Add a heaped teaspoonful of sugar, a small teaspoonful of made mustard and salt and pepper to taste. Stir till thick, and then pour over.

Menu 45

Mushroom Soup

Chop up half a pound of wild mushrooms and cook for twenty minutes with a sliced onion in a pint of white stock. Then rub through a sieve and reheat.

In another saucepan cook an ounce of flour with one and a half ounces of butter and, when smooth, add to it a quarter of a pint of cream.

Then add the soup to it and season well with salt, pepper and a little mushroom ketchup.

Pour into a thermos very hot.

Roman Pie

Line a charlotte mould with short crust and put in a paper filled with rice to keep a shape. When cooked, remove rice and paper and fill with the following mixture:

Chicken chopped small, macaroni boiled and cut up small, two boiled eggs chopped small, chopped parsley, salt, pepper, and a good white sauce.

Put back in oven to get hot. Turn out and serve. Put on pastry lid before baking.

Caraway Cheese

Mix with a cream cheese enough olive oil to make a paste and then half a teaspoonful of salt and a few grains of cayenne, a teaspoonful of caraway seeds pounded in a mortar, half a teaspoonful of finely chopped chives and a very tiny bit of minced onion.

Menu 46

Devilled Crab

Prepare the meat of a boiled crab by flaking it and add to it a quarter of a pint of béchamel sauce, a dessertspoonful of anchovy essence, a teaspoonful of Chili vinegar, a dessert-spoonful of chutney, a teaspoonful of made mustard and salt, pepper and cayenne.

Put it back into the shell, cover with breadcrumbs and bake in the oven for about fifteen minutes.

Serve cold.

Beef Salad

Take some thin slices of cold roast beef and cover them with chopped gherkins and chopped hard-boiled eggs. Then spread over the top a nasturtium sauce made as follows:

Melt three tablespoonfuls of butter and add the same of flour, mixing into a smooth paste. Season with salt and pepper, add one and a half cups of water and cook till thick, stirring carefully; then add gradually another three tablespoonfuls of butter and three tablespoonfuls of nasturtium seeds either pickled or fresh. Sprinkle finely chopped parsley over the top and the finely chopped yolk of an egg. Decorate the dish with slices of cucumber and gherkin.

Pimento Salad

Choose green and red capsicums. Mince them, or cut them into pieces and use either tinned or fresh pimentos.

Cover with oil and vinegar, seasoned with a little salt.

Marmalade Tart

Line a plate with pastry, cook it; fill it with Oxford marmalade, and put back into the oven for a few minutes.

Menu 47

Prawn Salad

1 tin of curried prawns or fresh prawns curried, 1 large lettuce, 1 glass of claret, 1 dessertspoonful of wine vinegar, 2 hard-boiled eggs, 1 teaspoonful of chutney, mustard and cress.

Tear up a lettuce and mix it with the mustard and cress.
Heap it up on a dish and arrange the eggs hard boiled and
cut lengthways in four round the salad. Make a ring of the
prawns outside all and sprinkle with a dressing made of the
claret, vinegar and chutney.

Serve with brown bread and butter.

Mutton Pies

Cut up some cold cooked mutton into dice. Fry some
onions in butter with a chopped bay leaf, a tablespoonful
of Harvey's sauce and a tablespoonful of Lea & Perrin's
Worcester sauce, four peppercorns, salt and pepper and
some chopped mushrooms.

Cook the mutton in these ingredients for twenty minutes and see that they are highly seasoned. Then make some
puff pastry, fill some tartlets with it, place the mixture inside,
cover with a lid of pastry, fluting the edge of each with a
knife. With a paste brush, brush them over with egg and
bake a nice brown. Serve cold.

Purée of Peppers

Cut in half twelve red peppers and twelve green and remove
all seeds. Then chop up the peppers with twelve onions very

fine and pour some boiling water over them.

Let them stand for five minutes. Drain, add four level tablespoonfuls of salt; bring to boiling point a cupful of sugar and one and a half pints of vinegar. Then boil for five minutes and fill jars.

Bananas with Rum

Peel the bananas, allowing one and a half for each person. Slice them lengthways and put them into a fireproof dish with a few tablespoonfuls of water. Sprinkle them with demerara sugar and the juice of a lemon and put in the oven for about ten minutes.

When cooked, pour a wineglass of rum over them and cover with whipped cream flavoured with lemon rind.

Menu 48

Mousse of Haddock

Remove the flesh of one or more smoked haddocks, pick out
the skin and bone; chop it finely and season with cayenne,
chopped parsley and mix it with a little butter and several
tablespoonfuls of cream. Stir over a gentle heat till thoroughly hot, add a few drops of lemon juice. Remove from
the fire and add the whipped whites of three eggs and put
into a wetted mould.

Avocado Pears

Halve the pears lengthways. Remove the stones and dress
with oil and vinegar.

Serve half a pear to each person.

Devilled Chicken

Cook the chicken and divide it into nice pieces. Then make
the following white devil:

Take half a tablespoonful of flour, a quarter of a tablespoonful
of English mustard, half a pound of butter, three-quarters of

a pint of cream, a little Harvey sauce and the same of Lea & Perrin's Worcester sauce, and salt, pepper and cayenne to taste.

Put all the ingredients in a saucepan and boil for five minutes, stirring continuously. Warm up the chicken in it and pour into a waxed container and leave to get cold before putting on the lid.

Tomato Jelly

Cook several pounds of tomatoes with a clove, a few leaves of tarragon, a coffeespoonful of chopped onions, a little sugar, pepper and salt. When tender, press out the juice through muslin.

To every pint of juice add half an ounce of melted gelatine. Stir until the mixture begins to cool. Pour into a mould and set in the refrigerator.

Menu 49

Fishchowder Soup

Slice two onions finely and fry in butter; slice in the same way four potatoes and fry with the onions. Add a cupful of tomato pulp, two pounds of fresh cod or other fish cut in cubes, four peppercorns, pepper and salt to taste and a quart of good stock.

Cook slowly in a casserole for about four hours.

Serve very hot.

Spiced Loaf

Mince six or eight ounces of raw meat and any remains of mutton, ham, cold beef or cold bacon and pass through a mincing machine.

When minced put it into a mixing bowl with three or four

uncooked sausages from which the skin has been removed.

Knead the whole well and add plenty of black pepper, salt, cayenne and seasoning, some finely chopped lemon rind, and a little powdered mace. Mix thoroughly; roll on a board which has been floured, make a nest for one or two chopped hard-boiled eggs, then roll the meat lightly over the eggs and make it into the form of a loaf. Flour a cloth, place the loaf in it and boil for one and a half hours.

When cooked, take out of the cloth and dip it in bread-crumbs so that the whole loaf is covered.

Glazed Cucumber

See page 27.

Cream of Tapioca

Boil two tablespoonfuls of Groult's tapioca in a pint of milk in a double saucepan very slowly for several hours, flavour with a few thin pieces of lemon rind and sweeten to taste.

When cold, whip into it a few tablespoonfuls of cream.

Serve separately with a dish of stewed red currants.

Menu 50

Mousse of Eggs

Hard boil four eggs, pass the yolks through a sieve and add three tablespoonfuls of aspic jelly or three sheets of gelatine dissolved, salt, pepper, Lea & Perrin's Worcester sauce and anchovy sauce to taste. Chop the whites and add them. Half whip half a pint of cream and add this. Put into a soufflé dish, and put in the refrigerator. Run a little aspic over the top. Decorate with tarragon, white of egg, a little more jelly, and let it set.

Turn out and surround with slices of cucumber.

Smoked Sausages

Choose a variety of smoked sausages, such as Swedish sausage and salami, and cut into slices with gherkins in between and round the dish.

Sauerkraut

Remove the outside leaves of one or more cabbages and then finely shred the head.

Line the bottom of a small wooden bucket with the discarded outside leaves and then place in a layer of the shredded cabbage and cover it with salt. Repeat until the bucket is full, pounding down well with a wooden mallet. Sprinkle salt over the top and cover with the large discarded leaves, and then with a cheese cloth wrung out in salt water. Tuck in the ends carefully and then place a board on the kraut and a heavy weight on that. The cabbage must be covered with brine. Remove the scum as it rises to the top.

In six weeks the kraut will be ready and it must be kept in a very cool place.

To bottle the kraut for preserving, fill jars with it and then fill up to the brim with boiling water. Seal them without screwing tightly and put in a hot water bath for an hour, then remove and seal securely. Store in a dry cool place.

Stuffed Olives

Take one ounce of tunny fish, one ounce of anchovies, half an ounce of large black olives. Pound well in a mortar and mix into a paste. Strain and add a little mustard, and two teaspoonfuls of olive oil. Take the stones out of the olives and fill with the mixture.

Apple Pie

Peel, quarter and core a pound of juicy cooking apples. Place in a deep dish, sprinkle them with half a cupful of granulated sugar, half a teaspoonful of spice and a level tablespoonful of butter dotted over them. Add two tablespoonfuls of water.

Cover with a good short pastry, put into a quick oven, brown, and then place on the lower shelf of the oven to let the apples cook to a pulp.

Remove from the oven, sprinkle with castor sugar and serve with thick cream.

Menu 51

Truite au Bleu

Place a small salmon trout in a fireproof dish and cover. Parboil some small sliced onions and carrots and add them together with five bay leaves, a little sugar, salt, and some peppercorns. Cover and bake in the oven. Allow to cool and garnish with bay leaves arranged across the fish and a spray of nasturtium leaves with flower at the head and tail. Surround with sliced cucumber.

Indian Pie

Mince two pounds of meat, soak a large slice of bread in a cup of milk, and squeeze it out. Fry two onions.

Mix all the ingredients and add a tablespoonful of curry powder, a dessertspoonful of sugar, the juice of a lemon and finally an egg. Whisk separately a second egg with a little milk and pour over the whole after putting into a pie dish. Bake in the oven and serve with blanched almonds stuck over the top, and a dish of boiled Patna rice.

Apple Soufflé

Peel and cut up a pound of good eating apples and cook them with the thin rind of half a lemon, sugar and a little water. When soft, pound them and put through a sieve to make a purée.

Then add the yolks of two eggs and cook for one minute, stirring carefully. When nearly cold fold in the stiffly beaten whites of four eggs.

Cook in a moderate oven in a soufflé dish standing in a basin of water.

Menu 52

Asparagus in French Rolls

Cut a small piece out of the top of as many French rolls as are required, and take out all the crumb. The piece that has been removed from the crust will have to be returned later. Fry the rolls a golden brown in butter.

Take the yolks of three eggs and beat them well with salt and pepper, and then stir in half a pint of cream and half a pint of milk. Mix in a double saucepan over the fire, stirring well till it thickens. Have the asparagus already cooked, put on one side twice as many as there are rolls. Cut the heads off the others, put them into the cream and fill the loaves with them.

Cold Grouse

Cook the grouse in the usual way, divide it up into tidy pieces and arrange on a dish, decorating with watercress.

Pickled Plums

Boil two and a half pounds of vinegar with three pounds of white sugar; then wipe the Victoria plums so that they are quite dry, put them in an enamelled bowl after pricking them, and pour the hot vinegar and sugar over them.

Leave them for two days, then pour off the vinegar, and boil it again and pour it over the plums and after two more days boil it again with half an ounce of cinnamon and some cloves. When the plums begin to burst it is done.

Lettuce and Cucumber Salad

See page 38.

Caramel Soufflé

Put a quarter of a pound of brown sugar into a pan with a tablespoonful of hot water and two ounces of butter.

Boil till thick, then cool. Melt another ounce of butter and add three ounces of flour and half a pint of milk and boil for a few minutes, stirring well. Then add the yolk of an egg and an ounce of almonds and cook for a few minutes. Take it off the fire and add the sugar mixture, stirring till dissolved. Melt a quarter of an ounce of gelatine in hot water and strain it into the mixture. When beginning to set, fold in the stiffly beaten whites of two eggs. Turn out and serve with baked chopped almonds on top.

Menu 53

Faggot Loaves

Beat up two eggs and make into a batter with two table-spoonfuls of flour and a little milk. Add seasoning and herbs. Mince half a pound of raw liver, two medium-sized onions and two rashers of bacon; soak two or three slices of bread in milk and mix all the ingredients together and add them to the batter, mixing well.

Put into greased tins with covers and stand them in a pan of water in the oven for under an hour.

Serve cold in slices.

Cold Daube of Lamb

Take a small leg of mutton, weighing if possible not more than four pounds. Bone it and trim it and rub it all over with salt, pepper and a pinch of cinnamon and ground cloves.

Leave it to marinate for one day in a tumblerful of white wine, a small glass of vinegar, some coarsely ground rock salt, a bouquet of herbs, pepper, and sliced onions and carrots.

The lamb should be almost covered, and turned from time to time. Round the meat should be put the bones, trimmings and a calf's foot cut in pieces.

Remodel the meat and tie it and put into a saucepan, resting on the carrots and onions; add the pieces of calf's foot and the marinade and, if this is not enough to cover the meat, add a little stock.

Cook very slowly for from six to seven hours.

Then remove the string, put the lamb in a deep dish and strain over it the gravy after carefully removing the fat, vegetables, etc. Leave it to get cold and the gravy should be a jelly.

Serve with spiced prunes.

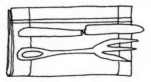

Spiced Prunes

Place a pound of prunes which have been soaked overnight and stoned in a casserole with a cup of water, a cup of brown sugar, a quarter of a cup of vinegar, half a stick of cinnamon, six cloves, four allspice, two blades of mace and half a teaspoonful of nutmeg. Let them cook very slowly till tender, then drain the syrup and boil it for ten minutes before pouring over the prunes.

Leave to get cold, and serve with the meat.

Salad of Pineapple and Grapefruit

Peel the fruit and flake it with a silver fork. Powder slightly with castor sugar and dress with oil and vinegar. Sprinkle with powdered nuts.

Strawberry Short Cake

Sieve together half a pound of flour, two teaspoonfuls of baking powder and half a teaspoonful of salt, and rub in two ounces of butter. Then add gradually enough milk to make into a dough. Toss it onto a floured board and divide it into two parts. Form each part into a flat round cake, and put each on a greased sandwich tin and bake in a hot oven at

450 degrees F. for fifteen minutes. Split them open, and butter them, and then fill with the strawberries prepared as follows:

Wash and take off the stalks from one and a half pounds of strawberries and leave a few whole on one side. Mash the rest and add enough white sugar to sweeten well. Leave it till all the sugar is dissolved; then cover one of the layers with this and put the other layer on top and put more of the strawberries on the top of the cake. Cover with whipped cream and decorate with the whole strawberries that were left for this purpose.

Menu 54

Cold Vegetable Soup

Boil half a pound of spinach, half a pound of sorrel and half a pound of beetroot leaves in salt water. When tender, strain and put through a sieve. Moisten the purée with a pint of "Kwas" or dry cider diluted with water. Add a little dill, tarragon, a pinch of salt and a tablespoonful of sugar. Cut two gherkins in slices, place in the tureen and pour the soup over them. Place in a refrigerator and, if possible, serve with ice in the soup.

Kwas

Boil six quarts of water and, when tepid, add an ounce of yeast, a bottle of light beer, half a pound of sugar and the juice of a lemon. Pour into bottles, leaving a third of each bottle empty, and distribute the finely peeled lemon rind amongst them.

Cork well, put overnight in a warm place. Then cool it down and, though ready for lunch, it will keep a week.

Cold Pheasant with Slices of Foie Gras

Cook the pheasant in the usual way and, when cold, divide into neat pieces.

Arrange on a dish with watercress in between and round the dish.

Serve the foie gras cut in slices on a bed of lettuce in a separate dish. If foie gras is too expensive, a chicken liver terrine can be used instead. This can be made at home according to the recipe given on page 26.

Banana Ice Cream

Place in a bowl one and a half cupfuls of banana pulp, a cupful of sugar and the juice of a lemon. Cover and leave. Then put in a saucepan a pint and a half of milk and four tablespoonfuls of cornflour. Stir into a paste and go on stirring till it thickens, and cook for five minutes. Add the yolks of two eggs, beat, add the banana and beat well again. Then beat into the mixture the stiffly beaten whites of two eggs. Put in the ice machine.

It makes about three pints of ice cream.

Menu 55

Pâté de Volaille

Bone a chicken and put the white meat on one side. Mince the rest with half a pound of lean veal and the same of lean pork and a quarter of a pound of fat pork. Season well and add a few chopped truffles.

Take a jar and put in first a layer of the minced meat, then a very thin rasher of bacon, the white meat of the chicken and so on till the pot is full.

Cook for an hour and a quarter in a bain-marie in a moderate oven.

Vegetable Macédoine

See page 73.

Strawberry Soufflé

1 pound of strawberries, ½ pint of custard made with eggs, 10 leaves of gelatine.

Pass the fruit through a hair sieve; make a custard with the yolks of four eggs and melt the gelatine in the fruit juice.

When cold, mix all together.

Beat up the whites stiffly and fold into the mixture. Pour in a wetted mould to set.

Menu 56

Spiced Oysters

Take two dozen oysters and bring to the boil over the fire in their own liquid from the shells. Only let them scald for two minutes and then drain. Wash them in cold water, measure the liquid and strain it back into the saucepan.

To three-quarters of a cup of the liquid add one half cup of vinegar, one grated onion, one finely chopped green pepper, one bay leaf, a teaspoonful of salt, a teaspoonful and a half of paprika, three cloves, two allspice, and a tablespoonful of Worcester sauce. Bring to the boil, cook for ten minutes and pour it over the oysters which have been placed in glass jars. Seal and leave to set.

Chicken Cream

Boil a chicken, remove the meat from the bones and mince it several times. Mix it with two tablespoonfuls of butter and a quarter of a pint of cream. Season well and then put through a wire sieve and beat it well. Line a mould very lightly with spice and fill with the mixture.

Sweet Pepper Salad

Mince separately six sweet green peppers and a small onion. Mince also a tiny piece of crystallized ginger about the size of a hazel nut. Mix all together and dress with a French dressing made of lemon juice, olive oil, salt, pepper and mustard. To two and a half tablespoonfuls of oil, there should be one and a half of lemon juice.

Menu 57

Hot Beetroot Soup

Put four ounces of butter in a pan, melt it and add six ounces of minced onions, two minced leeks, and one ounce of celery minced. Fry till they begin to turn yellow, then add about eight ounces of finely shredded red cabbage and continue the frying, and add eight ounces of thinly sliced beetroot, fry a little longer and then add a quart of good clear broth; bring to the boil and simmer till all the vegetables are cooked. Then strain.

Now slice separately two ounces of beetroot very thin and add a small teaspoonful of vinegar, and put this at the last into the soup with a gill of cream.

Partridges in Cream

Cook the partridges for twenty minutes in butter and cool the butter with a glass of sherry. Cook till reduced to half, then add a glass of thick cream. Season and pour over the partridges.

Salad of Mint Leaves and Beans

Take some cold French beans and mix with them the inner leaves of small round lettuces with a good deal of the heart on them, and mint leaves, about a third of each. Dress with oil and vinegar and sprinkle with chopped olives and finely chopped hard-boiled egg.

Butterscotch Pie

Line a plate with pastry. Then put into a saucepan a cup of brown sugar and an ounce and a half of butter. Heat slowly and cook for three minutes.

Then put in a bowl one cup and a half of cold milk and add four level tablespoonfuls of cornflour. Stir till dissolved and add it to the sugar, stirring all the time till it has come to the boil and cooked for three minutes.

Cool and add one well-beaten egg. Then pour into the plate lined with pastry. The sugar must not be allowed to caramel. Bake in a quick oven.

Menu 58

Hot Piedmontese Soup

Soak two ounces of breadcrumbs in a pint of milk; stir till smooth and add half a pint of tomato purée, two ounces of grated cooked lentils, and four ounces of cooked onion, and a seasoning of pepper, salt and rosemary; if too thick, add a mixture of milk and broth in equal proportions.

Potato Salad

See page 42.

Caramel Nut Ice

Scald one pint of milk and add it slowly to three well-beaten eggs and go on stirring till the custard coats the spoon, and then add the caramel made by boiling a cup of sugar in half a cup of water and stirring it till it is a golden brown. After adding the caramel to the custard, add a quarter of a pound of nuts in toffee crushed with a rolling pin.

When the ice mixture is quite cold, stir in a pint of stiff whipped cream and freeze.

Suitable Drinks

Beer will go excellently with any of the meals I have suggested, but if wine is preferred a white Anjou or a Chablis would be delicious with any of the menus containing fish. Sauterne also would be suitable for any or all of them, and claret if drunk after the fish.

Most Englishmen are happy with a good beer, and Bass No. 1 is an excellent bottled beer.

Many women like cider, and either Bulmer's or Gaymer's are good brands. Beer mixed with stone ginger beer makes an excellent drink called Shandy Gaff which is popular with men and women. The mixing must not be done beforehand.

Tea or coffee can be put hot into a thermos and will keep hot for many hours. The milk and sugar should be added when it is poured out.

Coffee must be an infusion of the freshly-ground berries, and a good blend is Costa Rica, East Indian and Mocha in equal proportions. A tablespoonful should be allowed for each coffee cup of water if it is to be drunk black after the meal, and a tablespoonful to each teacupful of water if it is to be café au lait.

If a liqueur is wanted, cherry brandy is a very appropriate one.

Packing the Picnic Basket

A SUITABLE picnic basket can be bought for 7s. 11d.

4 cups and saucers in Betel ware, 9d. each.

4 tea plates, 6d. each.

1 Betel sugar bowl with lid, 6d.

1 pepper in Betel, 3d.

1 salt in Betel, 3d.

8 cardboard plates, 6d.

A packet of waxed papers fluted at edge to fit them,
    1s. 6d. per gross.

4 tumblers, 8d.

4 teaspoons, 8d.

6 knives and forks, 3s.

6 dessertspoons, 3s.

6 waxed cardboard containers with lids, for cream, etc., 6d.

2 glass jars with screw lids, 1s.

1 glass dish for salad with spoon and fork, 1s.

1 wide mouthed thermos, 1½ pints, 11s. 6d.

1 ordinary thermos, 3s. 6d.

And, for those who can afford it, a thermos gallon ice-box with three containers for hot or cold food, £3, 15s. 6d.

Index

Acknowledgements

I gratefully acknowledge the permission I have obtained from the following publishers and authors to quote certain recipes from their books:

Marcel Boulestin, *The Conduct of the Kitchen*.
Published by Messrs. Heinemann.

Ambrose Heath, *Good Food*.
Published by Messrs. Faber & Faber.

K. and M. von Schumacher and P. and L. Gratton
Esmonde, *Cook's Tour of European Kitchens*.
Published by Messrs. Chatto & Windus.

Also *The Gentle Art of Cookery*.
Published by Messrs. Chatto & Windus.